SUPER SIMPLE ENGINEERING PROJECTS

ENGINEER IT! TUNNEL PROJECTS

CAROLYN BERNHARDT

CONSULTING EDITOR, DIANE CRAIG, M.A./READING SPECIALIST

Super Sandcastle

An Imprint of Abdo Publishing
abdopublishing.com

abdopublishing.com

Published by Abdo Publishing, a division of ABDO, PO Box 398166, Minneapolis, Minnesota 55439.

Printed in the United States of America, North Mankato, Minnesota
062017
092017

THIS BOOK CONTAINS RECYCLED MATERIALS

Production: Mighty Media, Inc.
Editor: Liz Salzmann
Cover Photographs: Mighty Media, Inc.; Shutterstock
Interior Photographs: AP Images; Mighty Media, Inc.; Shutterstock

The following manufacturers/names appearing in this book are trademarks: Aleene's® Tacky Glue®, Crayola®, DAP® Kwik Seal Plus®, Elmer's® Glue-All™, Scotch®, Sharpie®

Publisher's Cataloging-in-Publication Data

Names: Bernhardt, Carolyn, author.
Title: Engineer it! tunnel projects / by Carolyn Bernhardt.
Other titles: Tunnel projects
Description: Minneapolis, MN : Abdo Publishing, 2018. | Series: Super simple engineering projects
Identifiers: LCCN 2016963088 | ISBN 9781532111273 (lib. bdg.) | ISBN 9781680789126 (ebook)
Subjects: LCSH: Tunnels--Juvenile literature. | Tunnels--Design and construction--Juvenile literature. | Civil engineering--Juvenile literature.
Classification: DDC 624--dc23
LC record available at http://lccn.loc.gov/2016963088

Super SandCastle™ books are created by a team of professional educators, reading specialists, and content developers around five essential components—phonemic awareness, phonics, vocabulary, text comprehension, and fluency—to assist young readers as they develop reading skills and strategies and increase their general knowledge. All books are written, reviewed, and leveled for guided reading and early reading intervention programs for use in shared, guided, and independent reading and writing activities to support a balanced approach to literacy instruction.

TO ADULT HELPERS

The projects in this title are fun and simple. There are just a few things to remember. Some projects require the use of sharp objects. Also, kids may be using messy materials such as glue or paint. Make sure they protect their clothes and work surfaces. Review the projects before starting, and be ready to assist when necessary.

KEY SYMBOL

Watch for this warning symbol in this book. Here is what it means.

SHARP!

You will be working with a sharp object. Get help!

CONTENTS

WHAT IS A TUNNEL?

A tunnel is an underground path. It is completely enclosed with an opening at each end. Tunnels have existed since ancient times.

Many of the oldest tunnels were aqueducts. Aqueducts moved water. Some aqueducts brought water to crops. Others took water away from swamps. Aqueducts also provided people with water for drinking, washing, and cooking.

AQUEDUCT IN ISRAEL
BUILT 2,000 YEARS AGO

AQUEDUCT IN PERU
BUILT 1,400 YEARS AGO

ANCIENT BABYLONIA

The Babylonians were an ancient civilization that existed where Iraq is today. Nearly 4,000 years ago, the Babylonians built the first tunnel that went under a river. It went under the Euphrates River in the city of Babylon. This tunnel connected the royal palace on one side with a temple on the other side. It was 3,000 feet (900 m) long, 12 feet (3.7 m) high, and 15 feet (4.6 m) wide.

HOW PEOPLE USE TUNNELS

There are many uses for tunnels. Besides moving water, these uses include mining, sewers, and **transportation**.

MINING

Miners dig tunnels to reach natural resources that are underground. These include coal, diamonds, and gold.

SEWERS

Sewers take used, dirty water called sewage away from homes and businesses. Long ago, this water flowed in **gutters** on the streets. But exposed sewage can make people sick. Today, sewage flows through underground tunnels. Tunnels help keep our towns clean and healthy.

TRANSPORTATION

Tunnels help with **transportation** in different ways. They allow **vehicles** to pass through **obstacles**, such as mountains and rivers. Tunnels also keep **traffic** from dividing up **urban** areas. Instead, **subways** use tunnels to go under cities.

BUILDING TUNNELS

Building any tunnel requires digging into the ground. But there are different ways to do this. The method used depends on the type of tunnel being built. It also depends on what the ground is made of.

One important tool is a tunnel boring machine (TBM). People started making TBMs in the 1800s. Many improvements have been made since then. Today's TBMs have a rotating wheel in the front. This cuts into the ground. There are different types of TBMs, including hard rock TBMs and soft ground TBMs.

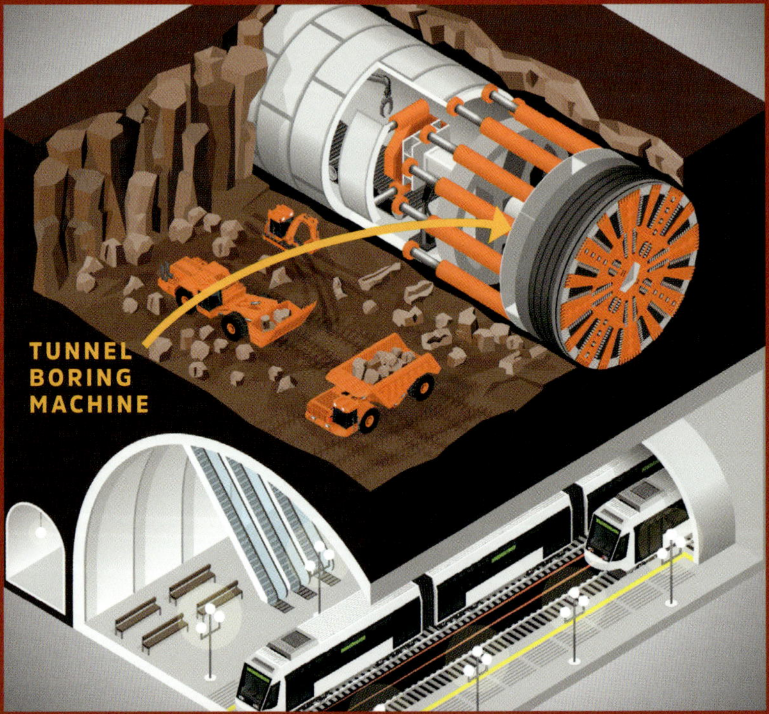

THE CHANNEL TUNNEL

The Channel Tunnel was completed in 1991. It goes under the English Channel between England and France. The tunnel is 31 miles (50 km) long. It takes about 35 minutes to travel through it. More than 23 miles (40 km) of the tunnel is actually under the channel. No other tunnel has an undersea portion that long.

TUNNEL STRUCTURE

When digging a tunnel, it's important to keep it from **collapsing**. Large tunnels are often dug from the top down. The top of the tunnel is dug out. This creates a bench. Then the bench is dug out. As the tunnel advances, workers add metal supports and a concrete shell. These make up the tunnel walls.

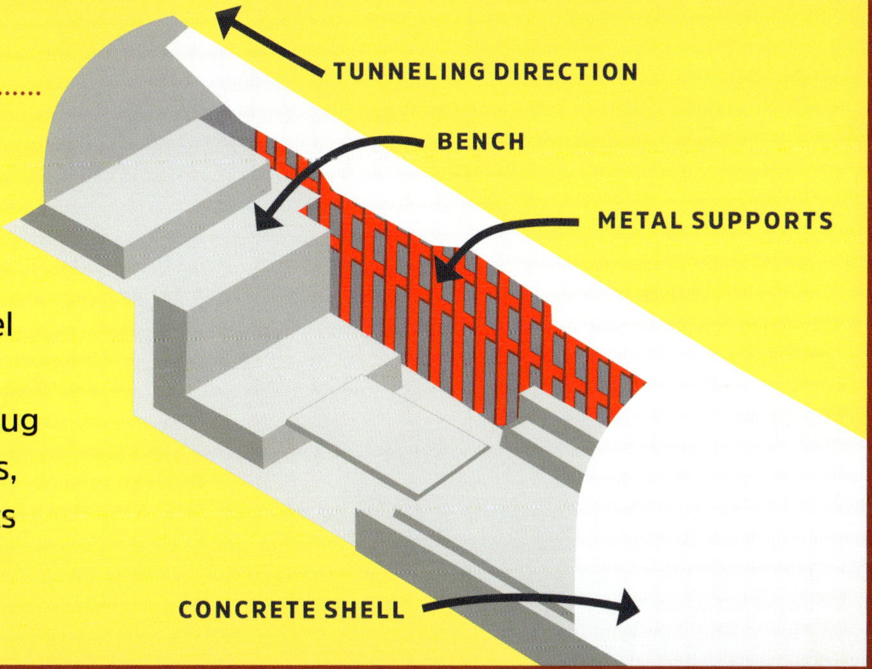

MATERIALS

Here are some of the materials that you will need for the projects in this book.

AIR-DRY CLAY

CARDBOARD

CHENILLE STEMS

CLEAR PLASTIC BOX

CLEAR PLASTIC JUG

CLEAR PLASTIC TUBING

CLEAR TAPE

CRAFT FOAM

CRAFT GLUE

CRAFT KNIFE

DOUBLE-SIDED TAPE

DUCT TAPE

FELT

FLORAL FOAM

FOOD COLORING

KITCHEN AND BATH ADHESIVE SEALANT

LARGE BEADS

LED STRING LIGHTS

MARBLES

PENCIL

PLASTIC CUP

RUBBER BANDS

SAND

SCREW

SERRATED KNIFE

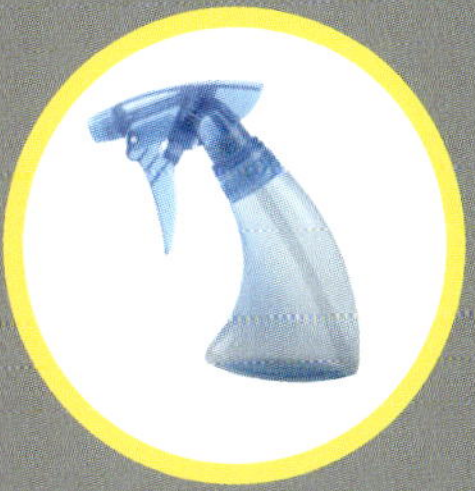

SPRAY BOTTLE

TENNIS BALL CANISTER

TOILET-PAPER TUBE

WOODEN CRAFT STICKS

WOODEN SKEWERS

UNDERSEA TUNNEL

MATERIALS: clear plastic jug, craft knife, clear plastic tubing, marker, kitchen and bath adhesive sealant, water, blue food coloring, toy car or train that fits inside the tubing, string

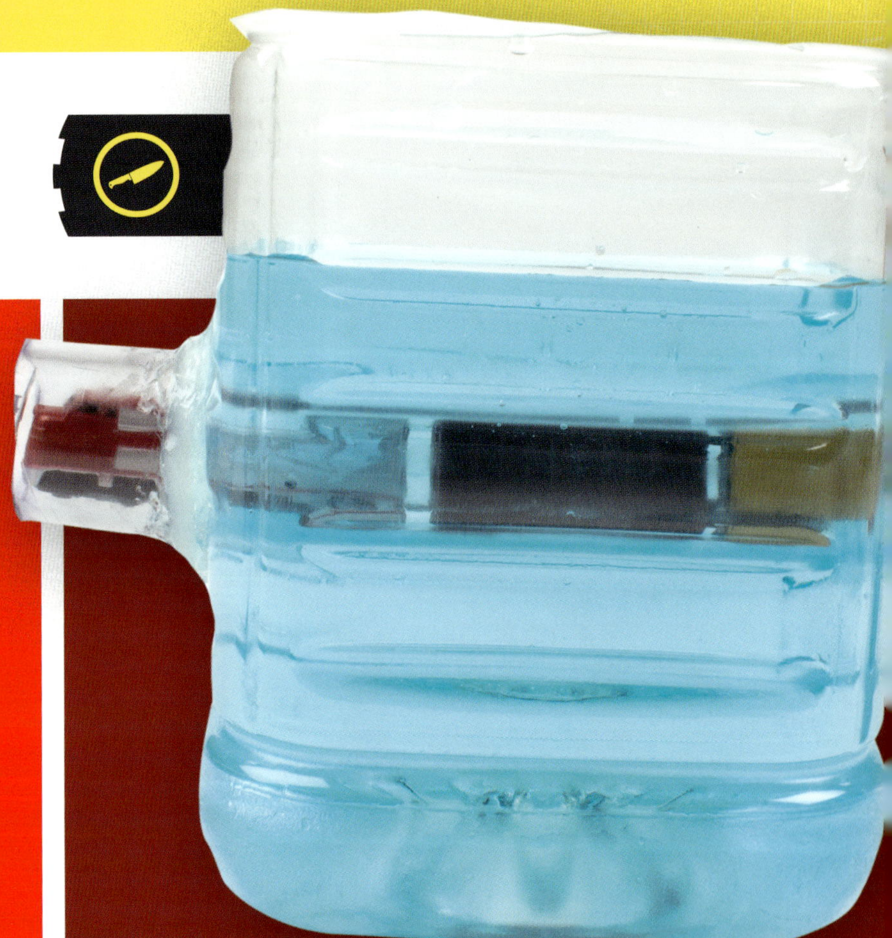

There are about 20 undersea tunnels around the world. A tunnel can sometimes be a better choice than a bridge. The body of water might be too wide for a bridge. Also, a bridge could block boat **traffic**. Tunnels are also less affected by the weather than bridges are.

1. Have an adult help you cut the top off the jug.

2. Press the end of the tubing against the side of the jug. Trace around it.

3. Have an adult help you cut out the circle you traced on the jug.

4. Push the tubing into the hole until it hits the other side of the jug. Trace the tubing on the outside of the jug. Have an adult help you cut out the circle.

5. Push the tubing through the second hole.

6. Use adhesive sealant to seal the cracks around both ends of the tubing. Let it dry.

7. Fill the bottle with water. Make sure it covers the tubing. Add two drops of blue food coloring.

8. Tie a piece of string to the front of the toy car or train. Use the string to pull the toy through your undersea tunnel!

TRAIN TUNNEL DESIGN

MATERIALS: large piece of cardboard, marker, toilet-paper tube, scissors, craft knife, air-dry clay, felt, double-sided tape, chenille stems, clear tape, toy animals and buildings (optional), toy train that fits inside the toilet-paper tube

Areas that have mountains often have tunnels too. A tunnel lets **traffic** go through a mountain instead of having to go over or around it. This is especially important for trains.

1. Draw your train's route on the cardboard.

2. Cut the toilet-paper tube in half **lengthwise**. Place the halves where you want tunnels to be.

3. Draw a line along each edge of both tubes. Have an adult help you cut **slits** in the cardboard where the lines are.

4. Push the edges of the tubes into the slits.

5. Create mountains on top of your tunnels with air-dry clay. Let the clay dry.

Continued on the next page.

TRAIN TUNNEL DESIGN (CONTINUED)

6 Cut shapes out of felt to make fields, lakes, or other features. Stick them to the cardboard with double-sided tape.

7 Cut treetops out of felt. Tape them to pieces of chenille stem to make trees.

8 Push the bottoms of the trees into the cardboard.

9 If you want to, decorate the scene with toy animals or buildings. Get creative!

10 Place your train on its track!

DIGGING DEEPER

Tunnels keep train tracks as flat and level as possible in areas that have mountains. This is necessary because trains are too heavy to travel easily up and down hills. All of the power moving a train comes from the engine in front pulling it. That's not too **difficult** on a level surface. But if the surface slopes up, it becomes much harder to pull the train. It's also hard to stop a train going downhill. If a train has to go up a hill, an extra engine may be added to help move the train. A particularly heavy train might need three or more engines!

TUNNEL

ONE ENGINE CAN PULL THE TRAIN THROUGH THE HILL

NO TUNNEL

TWO ENGINES NEEDED TO PULL THE TRAIN UP THE HILL

CUT-AND-COVER CONSTRUCTION

MATERIALS: tennis ball canister, craft knife, clear plastic box, clear tape, LED string lights, duct tape, sand, spray bottle, water, spoon, 2 large rubber bands, craft foam, scissors, small toys.

One method of building a tunnel is called cut-and-cover. It is used to construct tunnels in soft ground, such as clay or dirt.

1. Have an adult help you cut the tennis ball canister to fit in the box. The ends should press against the sides of the box.

2. Tape the string lights inside the canister.

3. Cover the edges of each end of the canister with duct tape. This is your tunnel.

4. Fill the box halfway with sand.

5. Spray the sand with water and stir it. Repeat until the sand is wet enough to stick together.

6. Dig a **trench** in the sand. Make it big enough to hold the tunnel.

Continued on the next page.

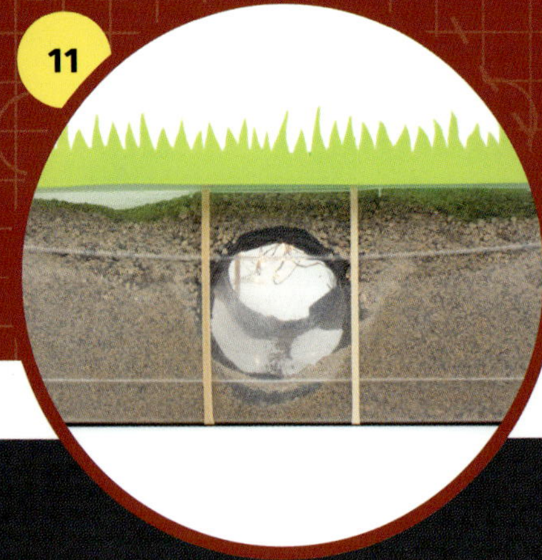

CUT-AND-COVER CONSTRUCTION (CONTINUED)

7 Place the tunnel in the **trench**. Make sure the lights are on top.

8 Wrap a rubber band around the box along each side of the tunnel. The rubber bands will hold the edges of the box against the ends of the tunnel.

9 Add more sand to cover the tunnel.

10 Put the lid on the box.

11 Create a surface over your tunnel. Cut grass out of craft foam. Add cars, people, or animals.

DIGGING DEEPER

Cut-and-cover is one of the oldest tunnel-building methods. Today, it is used for tunnels that don't need to be deep underground. **Subway** tunnels in cities are sometimes built this way.

First, workers dig a **trench** where the tunnel will be. Then they build the tunnel in the trench. Sometimes the tunnel is a tube that is constructed elsewhere and placed in the trench. When the tunnel is complete, the workers fill in the trench around the tunnel. Finally, they construct roads and buildings on the surface.

DIGGING THE TRENCH

BUILDING THE TUNNEL WALLS

COVERING THE TUNNEL AND BUILDING ON TOP OF IT

AMAZING AQUEDUCT

MATERIALS: cardboard, ruler, pencil, scissors, craft knife, marker, small wooden craft sticks, 2 large wooden craft sticks, craft glue, plastic cup, marbles

The Romans were very good at making water go where they wanted it to. They built aqueducts that moved water above and below ground.

2

3

5

1. Cut two cardboard rectangles that are the same size.

2. Use a ruler to draw a line at a slight angle along a long edge of one cardboard rectangle.

3. Draw a line in pencil ¾ inch (2 cm) below the first line. Erase ½ inch (1.3 cm) of the line from each end.

4. Carefully use the craft knife to cut a **slit** along the line you drew in step 3.

5. Use a marker to draw two more lines below the slit. Fill in the space below the lines with a brick wall pattern. Draw three archways.

Continued on the next page.

AMAZING AQUEDUCT (CONTINUED)

6 Cut along the line you drew in step 2.

7 Cut out the archways. This completes one wall of your aqueduct.

8 Repeat steps 2 through 4 with the second cardboard rectangle.

9 Turn the second cardboard rectangle over. Repeat steps 5 through 7 to complete the second aqueduct wall.

10 Set one wall on the table. Place short craft sticks side by side along the top of the wall. They should extend from one end of the **slit** to the other.

11 Cut the large craft sticks to fit across the row of small craft sticks. Glue them to the small craft sticks. Let the glue dry. This makes a bridge.

❶② Turn the craft stick bridge over. Fit the sides into the **slits** in the walls.

⑬ Place a cup at the lower end of the aqueduct. Gently drop marbles on the high end of the aqueduct. Watch them roll into the cup. This is how water flows down an aqueduct!

DIGGING DEEPER

An aqueduct system can include underground and above-ground sections. Above-ground, an aqueduct is like a combination of a tunnel and a bridge. The top of the structure has a covered channel for the water to flow through.

An aqueduct starts at a water source, such as a lake or river. Water from the source enters the aqueduct. It flows through the aqueduct to a **reservoir**. Then the water is piped to homes, businesses, farms, or wherever it is needed.

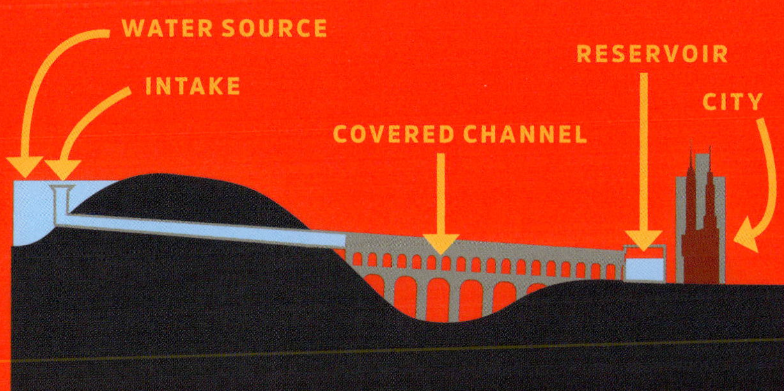

TBM

PUZZLE GAME

MATERIALS: newspaper, floral foam, large screw, serrated knife, wooden skewer, marker, bead or marble

Do you know how a tunnel is made? Engineers have invented giant machines that easily tear through the earth to leave behind a tunnel. They are called tunnel boring machines, or TBMs. These machines carve away the soil to begin building the tunnel!

2

4

5

1. Cover your work surface with newspaper.

2. Cut the floral foam so it's shorter than the large screw.

3. Push the skewer through the foam one or more times in one direction. Then twist the screw through the holes to make them larger.

4. Push the skewer through the foam one or more times in another direction. Each time, make sure you can see the skewer through at least one of the existing holes.

5. Enlarge the skewer holes with the screw.

6. Repeat steps 4 and 5 in the third direction. The block should now have several tunnels that cross each other.

Continued on the next page.

7

8

9

TBM PUZZLE GAME (CONTINUED)

7 Use the marker to write “START” over one of the holes.

8 Write a point value by each of the other holes.

9 Place a bead in the "START" hole. **Tilt** the foam to direct the bead through the tunnel system. Score the point value of the hole the bead comes out.

10 Take turns with your friends. See who can get the highest score!

DIGGING DEEPER

TBMs can be huge! The biggest one ever made was called Bertha. Bertha was used to dig a 1.7-mile (2.7 km) tunnel under Seattle, Washington. Bertha was 326 feet (99 m) long and 57.5 feet (17.5 m) wide. It weighed 7,000 tons (6,350 t). Twenty-five people at a time worked inside Bertha to operate and maintain it.

CONCRETE PANEL
Curved concrete panels form the walls of the tunnel. They are added in short sections as the TBM digs the tunnel.

TRAILING GEAR
This is where supplies are stored. It also includes restrooms and a kitchen for the workers.

CUTTERHEAD
The front of the machine has hundreds of sharp teeth. They cut into the ground as the head rotates.

TUNNEL SHIELD
The shield protects the workers and equipment inside the machine. Without a shield, dirt, rocks, and water could fill the freshly dug area.

CONVEYOR BELT
The TBM has a conveyor belt that goes from the cutterhead to the back. As the cutterhead cuts into the ground, the belt carries the loose dirt and rock out of the tunnel.

CONCLUSION

Tunnels are important structures that have many different uses. They provide direct routes for moving water, people, and goods. Engineers work to create strong, safe tunnels where they are most needed.

QUIZ

1 Aqueducts move water. **TRUE OR FALSE?**

2 The Channel Tunnel connects which countries?

3 What type of tunnel construction uses **trenches**?

LEARN MORE ABOUT IT!

You can find out more about tunnels all over the world at the library. Or you can ask an adult to help you **research** tunnels **online**.

Answers: 1. True 2. England and France 3. Cut-and-cover

GLOSSARY

collapse – to break apart and fall down.

difficult – hard to do, deal with, or understand.

gutter – a groove that catches and guides things.

lengthwise – in the direction of the longest side.

obstacle – something that you have to go over or around.

online – connected to the Internet.

research – to find out more about something.

reservoir – a natural or human-made place used for storing water.

slit – a narrow cut or opening.

subway – a system of trains that run underground.

tilt – to make something lean or tip to the side.

traffic – the cars, trucks, pedestrians, ships, or planes moving along a route.

transportation – the act of moving people and things.

trench – a long cut in the ground.

urban – of or related to a city.

vehicle – something used to carry persons or large objects. Examples include cars, trucks, boats, and bicycles.